THE CALL OF THE WILD

THE CALL
OF THE WILD

By Jack London

Adapted by Lillian Nordlicht
Illustrated by Juan Barberis

RSVP

**RAINTREE
STECK-VAUGHN**
P U B L I S H E R S
The Steck-Vaughn Company

Austin, Texas

Library of Congress Number: 79-24464

Library of Congress Cataloging-in-Publication Data

Nordlicht, Lillian.
  The call of the wild.

  SUMMARY: An unusual dog, part St. Bernard, part Scotch shepherd, is forcibly taken to Alaska where he eventually becomes leader of a wolf pack.
  [1. Dogs—Fiction. 2. Alaska—Fiction]
I. London, Jack, 1876-1916. Call of the wild.
II. Barberis, Juan Carlos. III. Title.
PZ7.N77547Cal   [Fic.]   79-24464

ISBN 0-8172-1656-1 hardcover library binding

ISBN 0-8114-6820-8 softcover binding

26   04 03

CONTENTS

INTO THE PRIMITIVE

1

The news spread quickly. "GOLD! GOLD!" Thousands of men rushed to the Northland. Dogs were needed to work for them; strong dogs with thick fur to keep out the frost. From Puget Sound to San Diego, such dogs were eyed with greed.

Four-year-old Buck did not know that trouble was brewing. Half St. Bernard, half Scotch shepherd, he was king of Judge Miller's estate in the Santa Clara Valley of California. Loved by the family, as was his father before him, his life was peaceful and contented.

One day Manuel, who worked in the garden and had a weakness for gambling, took Buck for a walk. No one saw them go. A stranger was waiting at the railroad station. Money changed hands.

"You might wrap up the goods before you deliver 'm," the stranger said.

Manuel doubled a rope. Buck accepted the rope Manuel tied around his neck. But when the rope was placed in the hands of the stranger, Buck sprang at him.

"Twist it, an' you'll choke 'm plentee," said Manuel.

Buck's breath was shut off. His strength ebbed. His eyes glazed. While he was unconscious, a train was flagged, and he was thrown into the baggage car.

When he came to, Buck fought bravely. But he could not free himself. During the fight, he bit the stranger.

The baggage man came to look into the sounds of the struggle.

"Yep, has fits," the stranger said, hiding his mangled hand. "I'm takin' 'm up for the boss to 'Frisco. A crack dog-doctor thinks that he can cure 'm."

When they reached San Francisco, the stranger took Buck to a shed in back of a saloon on the waterfront.

"All I get is fifty for it," he grumbled, "an' I wouldn't do it over for a thousand cold cash."

"How much did the other mug get?" asked the saloon-keeper.

"A hundred. Wouldn't take less, so help me," was the reply.

"That makes a hundred and fifty," the saloon-keeper said. "And he's worth it, or I'm a squarehead."

Buck tried to resist while the two men filed off his heavy brass collar. But he was choked into submission. Then he was flung into a cagelike crate.

In the morning, the crate was picked up by four men. Buck was carted off in a wagon. A truck carried him to a steamer. He was taken off the steamer to a railway depot. Finally he was left in an express car.

For two days and nights, Buck had nothing to eat or drink. Because he growled, he was teased and taunted and laughed at by men all along the way—just to humiliate him.

By the time he was delivered to a yard in Seattle, Buck was changed into a raging animal.

"You ain't going to take him out now?" the delivery man asked the stout man who signed for him.

"Sure," the stout man replied. Smiling, he reached for a hatchet and a club.

Everyone rushed for safety as the wood splintered.

"Now, you red-eyed devil!" said the man when Buck was free. He dropped the hatchet and shifted the club to his right hand.

Wild and starving, Buck hurled his one hundred and forty pound body at the stout man, only to be met by a blow that sent him crashing to the ground. He charged

more than a dozen times. Each time the club smashed him down. While he staggered limply about, the stout man dealt him a fierce blow on the nose. Buck crumpled up, knocked senseless.

When he opened his eyes, "Well, Buck, my boy," said the stout man. "You've learned your place. Be a good dog and all will go well. Be a bad dog, and I'll whale the stuffin' outa ya. Understand?"

While he spoke, the man fed Buck meat and water. Then he put him into a cage. Buck was beaten (he knew that); but he was not broken. He saw that he stood no chance with a man with a club. He faced that fact with all the hidden cunning of his nature aroused.

As the days went by, Buck saw other dogs taught the same lesson. A man with a club was a master to be obeyed.

He also saw men coming to look the dogs over. Sometimes money passed hands, and the dogs were taken away. Where did they go? Buck wondered. Why didn't they ever come back? He was glad each time when he was not chosen.

But his time came.

"Sacredam!!" cried a little man one day in broken English when he saw Buck. "Dat one 'am bully dog! Eh? How moch?"

"Three hundred, and a present at that," replied the stout man. "And seein' it's government money, you ain't got no kick coming, eh, Perrault?"

Perrault grinned. He knew Buck was "One in ten t'ousand!" he said to himself. The Canadian Government would do well by this purchase. Their dispatches would travel swiftly.

After Perrault bought Buck he bought a good-natured dog named Curly. Then he took them to the ship *Narwhal* where he turned them over to a half-breed named Francois.

Below deck, Buck and Curly joined two other dogs. One of them was a big white dog from Spitzbergen who smiled into Buck's face while he tried to sneak Buck's food at the first meal. The lash of Francois's whip reached him, and Buck was able to recover the bone. Although Buck was not fond of Perrault and Francois, he discovered that they were fair men, and he began to respect them.

The other dog he met was called Dave. Dave took an interest in nothing. All he wanted was to be left alone to sleep.

Day and night the ship throbbed and rolled and kicked and bucked, and the weather grew colder. At last one morning, the propellers were quiet. Francois brought the dogs on deck.

Buck's feet sank into something white and mushy and freezing. More of it was falling like rain. Buck licked some of it with his tongue. Instantly, it was gone. He sniffed more curiously, and the onlookers laughed uproariously. Buck felt ashamed. He didn't know why. It was his first snow.

THE LAW OF CLUB AND FANG

2

Buck's first day at Dyea Beach was a nightmare. He had come from a kind and gentle world. Here men and dogs were cruel and savage. He had already learned the law of the club. Now he was to learn the law of the fang.

Curly was the victim.

They were camped near the log store when she made friendly advances to the leader of a band of huskies.

In the wolf-manner of fighting, the dog leaped in and out, leaving Curly's face ripped wide open. Instantly, the rest of the band surrounded them, licking their lips.

Curly rushed the husky, only to be pushed back. Her next rush was met with a blow that tumbled her off her feet.

This is what the watching huskies had been waiting for, and they buried Curly under a mass of snarling, slashing bodies.

It happened so fast that Buck was taken aback. Francois, swinging an axe, tried to break it up. Three men with clubs helped him. In two minutes the dogs were driven off.

But Curly lay, limp and lifeless, in the bloody snow.

So that was the way it was. Once down, and that was the end of you. Buck vowed that he would see to it he never went down.

Spitz ran out his red tongue in the way he had of laughing. From that moment on, Buck hated him with an undying hatred.

Before Buck recovered from Curly's death, he got another shock. He was placed in a harness and put to work hauling a sled to the forest for firewood—just like the work horses back home. His pride and dignity were hurt. But he knew better than to protest.

Francois used his whip. Dave nipped his hindquarters. And Spitz jerked him the way he should go.

By the time they returned to camp, Buck knew enough to go at "MUSH!", to stop at "HO!", to swing wide at the bends, and to keep clear when the loaded sled shot downhill at their heels.

"T'ree vair good dogs," Francois told Perrault. "Dat Buck, heem pool lak hell. I tink heem queek as anyt'ing."

By afternoon, Perrault added three more dogs. They were good-natured Billee and his brother Joe, who was the very opposite. He also found an old, lean husky with one eye and a scarred face. He was called Sol-leks, which means The Angry One. Buck discovered that Sol-leks did not like to be approached on his blind side. Once he did and his shoulder was slashed to the bone. He never made that mistake again.

That night, a blizzard raged. The howling wind bit into Buck's wound. He tried to sleep in the tent. But Francois and Perrault chased him out.

He wandered sadly among the tents. Outside, no dogs were in sight. Where could they be? wondered Buck as he wandered about.

Something wriggled under his feet. He sprang back, snarling and afraid. A friendly little yelp calmed him and he went to look.

It was Billee, curled up in a snug ball under the snow. Buck dug a hole. The heat from his body filled the small space, and he slept soundly. Another lesson.

"Dat Buck for sure learn queek as anyt'ing," said Francois.

Perrault was happy he owned Buck. As courier for the Canadian Government bearing important dispatches, he tried to get the best dogs as he added three more. Then they were off, with Spitz leading.

Buck was surprised at the eagerness with which the whole team moved. They took delight in their work and the sled flew. The snow was packed and they made good time. But soon they had to make their own trail in the wilderness, and they were slowed down.

Buck had been put between Dave and Sol-leks in the traces so they might teach him. He was a quick learner; they enforced their teaching with nips from their sharp teeth. Once when he tangled the traces Dave and Sol-leks flew at him. The tangle became even worse, but Buck took good care to keep the traces clear thereafter.

It was a hard day's run, up the Canyon, past the timber line, across glaciers and snowdrifts hundreds of feet deep. They made good time down the chain of lakes which fills the craters of extinct volcanoes. Late that night they pulled into Camp Bennett, where thousands of gold seekers were building boats for the spring. Buck slept, exhausted, but all too soon was woken in the darkness and harnessed for another day's run.

For days unending, they broke camp in the dark, traveled many miles, ate their bit of fish, then crawled to sleep in the snow.

Buck was always hungry. Once a slow eater, he found that if he didn't finish first, he was robbed of his food by his teammates.

Hunger also turned him into a thief. When he saw one of the new dogs steal food, he did the same the following day. Then he stole whenever he could. This, more than anything, marked the change in Buck. Instincts long dead became alive again. The old tricks of his wolf ancestors were now his tricks, and he learned to fight with cut and slash.

His development was quick. His muscles became hard as iron, and he grew callous to ordinary pain. His sight and scent became very keen, while his hearing became so sharp that even in his sleep he could hear the slightest sound.

The tame generations fell from him. He seemed to remember the youth of his breed, when wild dogs ran in packs through the forest and killed their meat as they ran it down. And when, in the cold night, he pointed his nose at a star and howled, it was as if his ancestors howled through him.

All because men found gold in the North, and because Manuel, a gardener's helper, loved to play Chinese lottery.

THE PRIMITIVE BEAST

3

The cunning beast in Buck grew stronger and stronger, thanks to the fierce conditions of trail life. But it was a secret growth because he avoided fights.

Spitz's instinct told him that Buck was a threat to his leadership. Only a fight to the death of one or the other would end it.

This battle might have taken place early in the trip hadn't fate stepped in.

One day, they were forced by an Arctic storm to make camp. Buck found a sheltered place under a rock. Snug and warm, he almost hated to leave when Francois called him to supper. When he returned, he found Spitz in his nest.

Up until now Buck had avoided trouble with his enemy. But this was too much! He sprang upon Spitz with a fury which surprised them both. They circled around each other, cautious, but eager to fight.

"A-a-ah! Gif it to heem!" Perrault cried to Buck. "Gif it to heem, the dirty teef!"

Before Buck could, a band of about fifty huskies from a nearby Indian village appeared. Crazed by the smell of food, they buried their heads in the grub-box.

Perrault and Francois tried to club them, but the hungry pack ignored the rain of blows.

The noise awakened the sleeping team-dogs who burst out of their nests in surprise, only to be attacked by the fierce invaders. There was no opposing them. By the time they were driven off, all of the sled-dogs were wounded.

During the fight Spitz had rushed Buck, hoping to overthrow him. But Buck had braced himself and he was not successful.

From then on it was open war between them.

After Perrault and Francois dressed the dogs' wounds they pushed on to make up for lost time. It was important to get to Dawson as soon as they could. But the going was rough.

Once the sled broke through the thin ice and the dogs almost drowned before they were rescued. Frozen stiff, a fire had to be made to thaw them out.

Another time a glacier blocked their way. Perrault climbed it. Then with a long rope, he pulled the dogs, the sled, and Francois one by one, to the cliff crest. He was fearless! That was why he had been picked as a Government courier.

Buck's feet were not so hard as the feet of the huskies. All day long he limped in agony. When camp was made he would lie down like a dead dog. To help him Francois gave up the top of his own moccasins to make four little moccasins for Buck. This was a great relief, and even Perrault had to grin one morning when Francois forgot the moccasins and Buck lay on his back and waved his feet in the air. Later his feet grew hard, and the shoes were thrown away.

At last they reached their destination one dreary afternoon. They rested seven days. Then they were on their way again. Important dispatches had to be delivered. Besides, Perrault had made up his mind to set a record for speed this trip. He pushed the dogs mercilessly.

So determined was he, and so hard did he push them, that one of the dogs went mad. Dolly, who had never done anything odd, suddenly threw back her head and howled. Then she sprang straight for Buck. Buck fled from the scene in panic. He had never seen a dog go mad! He raced away with Dolly, panting, just one step behind. Francois called

to him, far away, and he doubled back, gasping for air. As they ran into camp Francois brought an axe down on mad Dolly's head.

Buck leaned against the sled, exhausted. Seeing his weakened condition, Spitz sank his teeth into Buck . . . and received the worst whipping any dog ever got from Francois.

Then and there Buck made up his mind he wanted the leadership and he openly defied Spitz. He no longer moved with the team as one. He encouraged the sled-dogs to all kinds of mischief. He also shrewdly managed to have Spitz punished for many of his own offences.

The fight for supremacy came about in a most unexpected way.

They had just made camp and settled down when a white rabbit flashed by. Buck had an instinct to kill, and with a happiness he had never known before, he led the team in a chase through the moonlight to run the rabbit down. Fifty huskies from a camp of the Northwest Police also joined the chase. Buck led the pack through the moonlight, around bend after bend, driven by the old joy of the hunt.

No one noticed Spitz take a short cut, and he reached the rabbit before anyone else did. Then he broke its neck.

Roaring with fury, Buck charged Spitz. But Spitz was an experienced fighter. His teeth bit deeply into Buck's shoulder and he sent him staggering, streaming with blood. In a flash, Buck knew it. The time had come. It was to the death.

The team had finished with the rabbit. Now they circled the fighters, waiting for one of them to go down.

Spitz was a practiced fighter. Through the Arctic and across Canada he had held his own with all kinds of dogs. Buck tried again and again to sink his teeth into the neck of the big white dog, only to be met with fangs. Over and over he rushed him, only to be slashed as Spitz leaped lightly away. Spitz was untouched, while Buck was panting hard. The fight was growing desperate. But Buck had a quality that made for greatness—imagination. He fought by instinct, but he could fight by head as well.

He rushed, as if trying the old shoulder trick. Then with a sudden change of pace, at the very last instant he swept low and closed his teeth on Spitz's left foreleg. Repeating the trick, he then broke the right one.

The quivering circle of sixty dogs started up. Struggling madly, Spitz disappeared from view under the mass of dogs.

Buck stood and looked on. He was the successful champion! He was the primitive beast who had made his kill and found it good.

WHO HAS WON THE MASTERSHIP

4

When Francois discovered that Spitz was missing and he saw Buck's wounds, he guessed what had happened.

"Wot I say?" he said to Perrault. "I spik true w'en I say dat Buck two devils. Now we make good time. No more Spitz, no more trouble, sure."

But when Perrault tried to put Sol-leks, who was the most experienced dog, in the leader's position, Buck was furious. The leadership was his by right! He had earned it! Snarling and snapping, he drove Sol-leks off.

Francois was angry. "Now, by Gar, I feex you!" he cried, coming back with a heavy club in his hand.

Buck was afraid of the club, but he would not back down. An hour went by and he was still circling the camp.

"T'row down de club," Perrault commanded.

Buck trotted triumphantly into position.

"Mush!" ordered Francois, and Buck proudly led the team. His leadership was far better than Spitz's. Under Spitz the team had grown unruly. In no time at all Buck licked them back into shape. Now they leaped as one dog in the traces.

"Nevaire such a dog as dat Buck!" cried Francois. "No nevair! Wot you say, Perrault?"

Perrault nodded. He was way ahead of schedule. They were making a record run. As they pulled into Skaguay, they were the center of a crowd of admirers.

For three days Perrault and Francois threw out their chests, and the men and dogs were treated royally. Then

24

came official orders. Francois and Perrault were transferred. Francois called Buck and threw his arms around him. He wept as he said goodbye. A Scotch half-breed took charge of Buck and his mates. That was the last they saw of Francois and Perrault.

With a dozen other dog-teams, Buck started back and forth between towns, with very little rest. The trips were difficult. Blizzards held them up. Solid sheets of ice wore them down. Soft snow meant a soft trail for the mail train. The drivers grumbled, but were fair. Each night the dogs were attended to first.

Buck's weight went down from one hundred and forty pounds to one hundred and fifteen. However, he bore up well to the work. But the rest of the team suffered greatly.

Billee cried in his sleep each night. Joe was sourer than ever. Sol-leks was unapproachable. But it was Dave who suffered the most. Something had gone wrong with him. Once out of harness it was hard for him to get up.

All of the drivers examined him. Then they talked his condition over at meal-time. They knew if a proud dog was denied work in the traces he would die.

Dave refused to run quietly on the trail behind the sled. He also bit the traces of any dog who was put in his place.

One night one of the men left the camp with Dave. A shot rang out. Buck knew, and every dog knew, what had taken place behind the river trees.

Buck and his teammates traveled twenty-five hundred miles in less than five months. They were tired and weary.

"Mush on, poor sore feet," their Scotch half-breed driver encouraged them. "Dis is the last. Den we get one long rest. For sure."

He expected a long stopover. But so many men had come to the Klondike that the mail was overwhelming. Officials ordered the worn-out dogs replaced with a fresh batch, and the others sold.

Charles and Hal, two men completely out of place in the North, bought Buck's team. Buck had an uneasy feeling

when he saw their dirty camp. It increased when Mercedes, who was Charles's wife and Hal's sister, ordered the packing.

Three men from a neighboring camp winked at each other as she insisted that the tent go on top of a mountainous load.

"I wouldn't tote that tent if I was you," they told her. "It's springtime. You won't get any more cold weather."

"However could I manage without a tent? Undreamed of!" she said.

Charles and Hal put more odds and ends on the load. Then "Mush," shouted Hal. "Mush on there!"

Nothing happened. The dog's muscles bulged, but the sled stayed put.

"Lazy brutes!" shouted Hal, lashing out with his whip.

"Those dogs need a rest. That's all that's wrong with them," said one of the onlookers, clenching his teeth. "I don't care what happens to you. But help the dogs. Break out the runners. The sled is frozen fast."

Hal and Charles threw their weight against the frozen runners, and the sled shot ahead. But the path twisted and sloped steeply. As the dogs swung on the turn, the sled went over, spilling half its load.

Buck broke into a run, happy to be free of Hal's whip. The team followed his lead. Kind-hearted people gathered up the scattered belongings. Then they caught the dogs and gave Hal advice.

"More dogs and half the load if you expect to reach Dawson."

Hal bought six more dogs.

"Most teams have eight," he boasted. "Think how fast we can go with fourteen!"

What he did not know was that one sled could not carry enough supplies for fourteen dogs. Before the trip was half over, they were short on food.

Then came the underfeeding, and the dogs began to die. Before long only five dogs were left. Arctic travel also

became too harsh for the two men and the woman. Mercedes insisted upon riding the sled, even though Charles and Hal begged her not to. They also began to quarrel among themselves about the share of the work.

Through it all, Buck staggered along at the head of the team. All the gloss was gone from his beautiful coat. His muscles were wasted to knotty strings. His bones were outlined clearly. Only his heart was unbreakable.

Unnoticed, each day ghostly winter was giving way to the spring awakening of life. Things were beginning to thaw and bend and snap. Sap was rising in the pines, squirrels were chattering, birds were singing, and the Yukon was struggling to break the ice that bound it.

Amid all this bursting of new life, they staggered into John Thornton's camp at the mouth of White River. While they rested, Hal told John Thornton about their trip.

"They said we couldn't make White River because of the melting ice, and here we are!" he finished up triumphantly.

"And they told you true," John Thornton answered. "Only the blind luck of fools could have made it. The bottom's likely to drop out at any moment. I wouldn't risk traveling on that ice for all the gold in Alaska."

"All the same, we'll go on to Dawson," said Hal, uncoiling his whip.

The team crawled to their feet. The lash bit Buck again, but he made no effort to get up. He had felt the thin ice under his feet. Even the heavy blows could not make him rise.

Suddenly, John Thornton hurled himself upon Hal. "If you strike that dog again, I'll kill you!" he cried.

"It's my dog," replied Hal, wiping the blood from his mouth. "Get out of my way, or I'll fix you. I'm going to Dawson." He drew his long hunting knife.

Thornton had no intention of getting out of the way. Mercedes screamed as he seized an axe handle, rapped Hal's knuckles, and knocked the knife to the ground. He rapped Hal's knuckles again as he tried to pick it up. Then stooping, he picked up the knife himself and with two strokes, cut Buck's traces.

Hal had no more fight left in him. Besides, Buck was too near dead to be of further use in hauling the sled. He pulled out from the bank and headed down the river.

Buck raised his head to see them go. Mercedes was riding the loaded sled. Charles was stumbling behind. The dogs were staggering.

Suddenly, a whole section of the ice gave way. Humans and dogs disappeared. A yawning hole was all to be seen. The bottom had dropped out of the trail.

Thornton knelt beside Buck. His rough kind hands searched for broken bones. "You poor devil," he said.

Buck licked his hand.

FOR THE LOVE OF A MAN

5

John Thornton had frozen his feet the previous December. His partners, leaving him to get well, went up the river to get a raft of saw-logs for Dawson.

Lying in the sun, he and Buck slowly won back their strength.

Skeet, Thornton's little Irish setter, quickly made friends with Buck. So did Nig, a good-natured black dog, and they had good times together.

But he still was a wild thing. He still fought as fiercely and shrewdly as ever. Not with Skeet and Nig, but with strange dogs.

In John Thornton, Buck found a kindness he had never known before. Not even with the Millers, back in the Santa Clara Valley. This man had saved his life. This man was the ideal master. Buck went wild with happiness whenever John Thornton touched him, and his love for the man grew stronger and stronger.

But deep in the forest, a call was sounding. Mysterious, thrilling and luring, it stirred Buck, and he would start up, sniffing the air. But so great was his love for John Thornton that it drew him back. Nothing was too great for Buck to do, when Thornton commanded.

One day a thoughtless whim seized Thornton.

"Watch this," he said to Hans and Pete, his partners.

Pointing to the crest of a cliff which fell straight down three hundred feet below, "Jump, Buck!" he commanded.

The next instant he was struggling with Buck on the

32

extreme edge, while Hans and Pete were dragging them back to safety.

"It's uncanny," said Pete, after he caught his breath. "I'm not hankering to be the man that lays hands on you while he's around."

"Py Jingo! Not mineself either," Hans agreed.

Before the year was up, Pete's fears came true at Circle City.

They were in a bar when "Black" Barton, an evil-tempered man, was trying to pick a quarrel with a tender-foot. Good-naturedly, Thornton tried to stop it. Without warning, Barton struck Thornton and sent him reeling.

Instantly, Buck's body rose in the air. As he aimed for Barton's throat, the crowd stepped in using clubs. Only that saved Barton. From that day on, Buck's fame spread through every camp in Alaska.

Later on, Buck saved John Thornton's life in quite another fashion.

The three partners were poling a boat down a bad stretch of rapids. Thornton was in the boat, shouting directions to the men on shore. Buck, keeping abreast, never took his eyes off his master.

The boat was flying downstream in a swift current when Hans checked the rope too suddenly. The boat turned over and flung Thornton downstream toward the worst part of the rapids, in which no swimmer could live.

Within seconds, Buck was in the mad swirl of water, and Thornton grasped his tail. But the current was so wild, Thornton knew that reaching shore was impossible.

Releasing Buck, "Go, Buck, go!" he shouted, pointing to shore while he clung to a slippery rock.

At Thornton's command, Buck swam obediently toward the bank, and was dragged ashore by Hans and Pete. Swiftly they tied the rope with which they had been snubbing the boat to Buck's neck and shoulders and launched him into the stream. He struck out boldly but was swept past Thornton. Hans and Pete pulled him back half-

drowned. While they were pounding the water out of him, they heard the faint sound of Thornton's voice.

It acted on Buck like an electric shock! Springing to his feet, Buck ran to the bank and waited to be launched again.

This time he headed in a straight line for Thornton. Thornton closed both arms around his shaggy neck. Hans snubbed the rope around the tree, and Buck and Thornton were jerked under the water as Pete and Hans hauled them in.

Both were nearly drowned. When Thornton came to, his first concern was for Buck, who had three broken ribs.

"We camp right here!" he announced. And they did, until Buck was able to travel.

That winter, Buck added another performance that put his name many notches higher on the totem pole of Alaskan fame.

In the Eldorado Saloon, three men were boasting about their favorite dogs. One man stated that his dog could start a sled with five hundred pounds. Another bragged six hundred for his dogs. A third, seven hundred.

"Pooh! Pooh!" said John Thornton. "Buck can start a thousand pounds."

"And walk with it for a hundred yards?" demanded Matthewson, the Bonanza King.

"Yes," said Thornton, coolly.

"Well, I've got a thousand dollars that says he can't. And there it is!" Matthewson slammed a sack of gold down upon the bar.

Half a ton! Thornton knew his tongue had tricked him. Never had he faced the possibility of Buck pulling such a load. Furthermore, he had no thousand dollars. Nor did Hans or Pete.

"I've got a sled outside now with twenty fifty-pound sacks of flour on it," said Matthewson, "so don't let that stop you."

Everyone was watching. Thornton had to do what he would never have dreamed of doing.

35

"Can you lend me a thousand?" he whispered to an old-time comrade.

"Sure," answered Jim O'Brien, thumping down a sack. "Though it's little faith I'm having, John, that the beast can do the trick."

Everyone ran outside.

Matthewson's sled, loaded with a thousand pounds of flour, had been standing for hours in the sixty-below-zero weather. The runners were frozen fast to the hard packed snow.

Odds of two to one were offered that Buck could not budge the sled. Someone upped them three to one against Buck. There were no takers.

"Three to one!" cried Matthewson. "I'll lay you another thousand at that figure, Thornton. What do you say?"

Although Thornton's doubts were strong, his fighting spirit was aroused. But all he, Hans, and Pete could raise was another two hundred dollars. Yet, he unhesitatingly bet this against Matthewson's six hundred.

Buck was in perfect condition. He felt the excitement as he was hitched to Matthewson's sled.

Thornton knelt down and whispered in Buck's ear. "As you love me, Buck. As you love me."

Buck seized his mittened hand between his jaws and squeezed it slowly in answer and love.

"Now, Buck, GEE!" Thornton commanded, stepping back.

Buck tightened and slacked the traces. The load quivered, and the ice cracked under the runners.

"Now, MUSH!"

Thornton's command cracked out like a pistol shot.

Buck lunged forward. His whole body gathered for the tremendous effort. His chest was low, his head was down, and his feet were flying like mad as he inched forward . . . half an inch . . . two inches. . .

At last he was gaining momentum, and he moved steadily along.

Thornton ran behind, encouraging Buck with cheery words. As Buck neared the end of the one hundred yards, the crowd burst into a roar. Hats and mitten went flying in the air. Even Matthewson shook hands. But Thornton fell on his knees beside Buck. Those who heard him, heard soft and loving words.

"Gad, sir! I'll give you a thousand for him. A thousand, sir—twelve hundred, sir," someone offered.

Thornton rose to his feet. Tears were streaming down his face. "Sir, you can go to the devil, sir," he said to the man. "It's the best I can do for you, sir."

THE SOUNDING OF THE CALL

6

The sixteen hundred dollars Buck won allowed John Thornton and his partners to follow a dream. They dreamed of finding a lost mine. Dying men who came out of the wilderness insisted it existed. So they traveled through the vast, uncharted Northland looking for gold.

John Thornton asked little of man or nature. He was unafraid of the wild. He hunted his food as he traveled, and if he failed to find it, he kept on traveling, knowing that sooner or later he would come to it.

Buck loved the hunting, fishing, and wandering through strange places.

For weeks at a time they would travel. Then for weeks they would camp. The dogs would rest and the men burn holes through frozen gravel and wash countless pans of dirt by the fire. Sometimes they went hungry, and sometimes they feasted. In summer they rafted down the rivers, and in fall they came to a sad lake country where there was no sign of life. Sometimes they saw the trail of men who had gone before them. Once they came upon a lost cabin in the wilderness. John Thornton found a long-barreled flintlock that belonged to the Hudson Bay Company when they hunted for beaver skins, but that was all. There was no sign of the man who had owned it.

Time went by. Then one day they found, not the lost mine, but a place in the valley where gold shone like yellow butter across the bottom of the washing-pan.

They looked no further.

Each day thousands of dollars in clean dust and nuggets were sacked in moosehide bags, fifty pounds to the bag.

There was nothing to do while the men gathered up the treasure.

Buck spent long hours by the fire. He was aware of wild yearnings and stirrings he could not explain. As he lay by the fire, he sometimes had visions of another life. He seemed to remember sitting by a fire with another man, short and hairy. The man slept restlessly, awakening often to stare into the darkness. At times Buck and the hairy man seemed to creep through a forest, both of them alert for danger. The hairy man could spring up into the trees and run along the branches, and Buck had memories of nights spent under the trees where the man slept.

Like these visions, calls from the depths of the forest filled him with unrest and strange desires. Sometimes he followed the call into the forest, looking for it as though it were something he could touch. He would run through the forest spaces or lie crouched behind logs, watching everything that moved around him.

One night he heard a long drawn-out howl. In some way he knew it as a sound that he had heard before.

Springing to his feet, he dashed through the sleeping camp to the forest. There he faced a timber wolf — who fled at the sight of him.

Buck overtook him easily, but the wolf escaped. Again Buck chased him. Then the wolf, finding that Buck did not wish to harm him, sniffed noses with him.

Old memories were coming back to Buck. He had done this some time before and now he was doing it again. Running free in the open, with the wide sky overhead.

When the wolf started back to the place he had come from, Buck started to follow him. Then stopped. He remembered John Thornton. He sat down. The wolf returned to him and made motions as though to encourage him. But Buck turned around and started slowly on the back track. For most of an hour his wild brother ran by his

side, whining softly. Then he sat down and howled. Buck held steadily on his way and heard the howl grow fainter and fainter until it was lost in the distance.

John Thornton was eating dinner when Buck dashed in and sprang on him in a frenzy of affection. Then for two days and nights he never left camp, or let Thornton out of his sight.

But two days later, the call sounded again. Buck's restlessness returned. He was haunted by memories of his wild brother, and he wandered for a week, looking for him. While he did, he fished for salmon, and killed his meat. He survived where only the strong survived, and it gave him great pride. His muscles were charged with vitality.

"Never was there such a dog," said John Thornton.

"When he was made the mold was broke," Pete added.

"Py Jingo! I t'ink so myself," agreed Hans.

What the men did not see was the terrible change that took place whenever Buck was in the secrecy of the forest. He truly was a thing of the wild. He crawled like a snake before he struck. He killed with delight and cunning. His lightning-like quickness combined with his intelligence made him as dangerous a creature as any that roamed the wilderness. He was a killer, a thing that preyed, living on the things that lived.

One day he came upon a moose herd. He had already dragged down a part-grown calf. But he felt like fighting. He sought out a huge bull with a vicious temper.

First Buck cut him off from the rest of the herd. Then he teased the bull by dancing before him. For four long days and nights, Buck never let his prey rest. He never gave him an opportunity to eat or drink. He would bark and dance about just out of reach of the great antlers and the terrible hooves. The bull was enraged, but try as he might, he could not rid himself of Buck. Buck followed him with all the patience of the wild. As the great head drooped more and more under its tree of horns, Buck showed no mercy. Finally, he killed him. Then he started back for camp.

Three miles away, he saw a fresh trail that made his hair bristle. Every nerve strained and tensed. A hundred yards further, he found a trail of dead sled-dogs, and he heard the sound of many voices rising in a chant. At the edge of the clearing, he found Hans, lying on his face, feathered with arrows like a porcupine.

A gust of overpowering rage swept over Buck. He did not know that he growled aloud. For the last time in his life he let anger overcome cunning and reason. Because of his great love for John Thornton he lost his head.

The Yeehats were dancing about in the wreckage of the lodge when they heard a fearful roar, and Buck, in a wild hurricane of fury, hurled himself upon them in a frenzy to destroy. He sprang at the chief of the Yeehats and ripped his throat open. Without pausing he jumped on the next man. There was no stopping him. He plunged through the Indians, tearing and destroying, defying the arrows that were shot at him. In fact, he moved so quickly that the Yeehats found themselves shooting each other instead of Buck.

So rapid were his movements, and so terrifying, that the Yeehats, sure the Evil Spirit was after them, fled to the woods! They scattered far and wide over the country. But not before Buck killed their chief by ripping his throat wide open.

Buck found Pete in his blankets where he had been killed, taken by surprise. Every detail of Thornton's desperate struggle was freshly written in the earth, down to the edge of a deep pool.

Buck brooded all day by the pool. John Thornton's death left a void in him that ached and ached, and which nothing could fill. At times he forgot the pain of it; and at such times he was aware of a great pride in himself — a pride greater than any he had yet felt. He had killed a man, the noblest game of all. It was strange — they had died so easily. It was harder to kill a husky dog than them. They were no match for him at all.

44

No longer would he be afraid of men except those holding spears and arrows and clubs in their hands.

Night came, and with it a full moon rose in the sky. From far away came the howls of the timber wolves.

Buck stood listening. John Thornton was dead. The last tie was broken. He was ready to answer the call.

The yelps grew closer and louder. Buck stood motionless, waiting.

The wolf pack poured into camp in a silvery flood in the moonlight — and the leader leaped straight for Buck. In a flash, Buck struck, breaking its neck. Three other wolves, one after the other, tried to meet him in battle. They, too, drew back, blood streaming from their slashed throats and shoulders. Gathering together, the pack tried to rush Buck. But snapping and gashing, he was everywhere at once. So well did he fight at the end of a half hour the wolves drew back. Their tongues were hanging out and they were panting. Some were lying down, while others were on their feet, watching him.

Then one lean gray wolf advanced. Buck recognized him from the forest. They whined softly, and touched noses.

Another wolf, old, gaunt and battle-scarred, howled a long wolf-howl of welcome. Buck howled back. When the leader sprang into the woods, Buck ran behind, yelping as he ran.

He was one with his wild brothers.

But the story does not end here.

Not too many years later, the Yeehats noticed a change in the breed of timber wolves. They had splashes of brown on their heads, and rifts of white down their chests.

More remarkable, the Yeehats told of a Ghost Dog that ran at the head of the pack. He had cunning greater than theirs, and he stole from their camps, robbed their traps, killed their dogs, and defied their bravest hunters.

He was a great, gloriously coated wolf, like and yet unlike the other wolves. He crossed from a certain valley

the Yeehats never entered, and came down to an open space among the trees. There a yellow stream flowed and rotted moose-hide sacks lay on the ground. Here, he mused for a time, howled once, long and mournfully, then departed.

He was not always alone. When the long winter nights came, and the wolves followed their meat into the valley, he could be seen running at the head of the pack, leaping gigantically above his fellows. And he sang a song of his world, which was the song of the pack.

GLOSSARY

ancestor (an′ ses′ tər)   one from whom someone is descended, as in a family

dispatch (dis pach′)   an important message

encourage (in kər′ ij)   to give hope or courage to someone

experience (iks pir′ ē əns)   the knowledge that is gained by doing a thing

husky (həs′ kē)   a strong dog with a thick coat, often used to pull sleds in the Arctic

imagination (i maj′ ə nā′ shən)   the ability to think of new things and deal with problems that have not been known before

instinct (in′ stingkt′)   a feeling or action that comes without being learned

struggle (strəg′ əl)   to make a great effort against difficulty

submission (səb mish′ ən)   the act of putting oneself under the control of someone else

supremacy (soo prem′ ə sē)   the position of highest power or rank

survive (sər vīv′)   to stay alive

wilderness (wil′ dər nəs)   a wild place where few or no people live